PLR PAYDAY

PLR
PAYDAY

Building Your Brand & Bringing in Bucks
With Private Label Rights!

JON J. CARDWELL

PLR Payday

Copyright © 2012 by Jon J. Cardwell. All rights reserved.

Cover design and internal art by Jon J. Cardwell © 2012.

Published by Vayahiy Press   vayahiypress.com

Printed in the United States of America

PLR PAYDAY
"BUILDING YOUR BRAND & BRINGING IN THE BUCKS WITH PRIVATE LABEL RIGHTS"

ALL RIGHTS RESERVED: No part of this book may be reproduced or transmitted in any form whatsoever, electronic, or mechanical, including photocopying, recording, or by any informational storage or retrieval system without express written permission from the copyright owner.

DISCLAIMER AND/OR LEGAL NOTICES: The information presented herein represents the view of the author as of the date of publication. It does not necessarily represent the view or marketing practices undertaken by the publisher. Because of the rate with which conditions change, the author reserves the right to alter and update his opinion based on the new conditions. All trademarks used are properties of their respective owners.

THE BOOK IS FOR INFORMATIONAL PURPOSES ONLY. While every attempt has been made to verify the information provided in this book, neither the author nor publisher assume any responsibility for errors, inaccuracies or omissions. Any slights of people or organizations are unintentional. Any reference to any person or business whether living or dead is purely coincidental. If advice concerning legal or related matters is needed, the services of a fully qualified professional should be sought. This book is not intended for use as a source of legal or accounting advice. You should be aware of any laws which govern business transactions or other business practices in your country and state.

TABLE OF CONTENTS

1. Let's Make Some Money Using PLR	1
2. All About Your PLR License	7
3. Create Top Quality Info Products	17
4. Seeking Quality Sources	31
5. Stepping It Up With Membership Sites	49
6. Maximize Your PLR Potential	55
7. Beef Up Your Product Value	59
8. Build Your List	61
9. Building Websites	63
10. Riding The Amazon Marketplace River	67
11. Reaping The Benefits Of Other Venues	91
12. Resounding A Promotional Voice	93
13. Recapping With Resources	97
14. Bibliography	103
15. About The Author	107

Let's Make Some Money Using PLR

Have you been struggling to make money online because you simply can't afford the hefty costs of outsourcing your projects?

For many, start-up costs are often the biggest obstacle standing in the way of getting their business online.

Just hiring an experienced writer to create a basic 50-page eBook can cost up to thousands of dollars; and that doesn't include all of the other components involved in building a high quality website that produces cash conversions. You would have to…

- 💲 Outsource copywriting to create high-converting sales pages

- $ Outsource to a designer to build you an attractive, attention-getting website

- $ Pay for a domain name and hosting account

- $ Create or outsource promotional material in order to recruit affiliates

- $ Create or outsource business development pros to fit all the pieces together with focused and synchronized precision marketing

Now, realizing all of that, what would you say if I told you that there's a simple solution that will instantly eliminate up to 99% of your start-up costs and, at the same time, give you the opportunity to build countless online businesses faster and easier than ever before?

You've no doubt heard the term "private label content" here and there as you've researched online businesses, but never knew what to do with it. Perhaps you've heard some things about it but never anything about just how powerful this resource really can be.

Or maybe you're someone just like me— caught in an economy that has forced you to seek employment apart from your regular call or vocation in order to make ends meet. That's

PLR PAYDAY

right; Internet marketing isn't my primary mission in life.

Hi, my name is Jon Cardwell and I'm a Baptist pastor and missionary whose primary call is to preach the gospel of Jesus Christ; yet, as government rollbacks, closures of military installations, and other elements of the economy have taken their toll on the small Alabama town where I now live, I found that at the age of 51 (I'm just about ready to turn 52 at the time of this writing), I needed to find some supplemental income, *and pronto*. Yet, because of the physical ailments I now suffer (after six years of symptoms that very closely resemble Lou Gehrig's disease: I may be on the verge of receiving a diagnosis from the VA— possibly PLS), the list of jobs and types of work I can perform has greatly been reduced.

Long gone are the days when I could run and jump and do pushups all day long like I could when I was a deep sea diver with the U.S. Navy. Gone are the days of missionary life in native villages of bush Alaska along the Bering Sea. In fact, because of my ailments, which present coordination problems and dexterity difficulties, I can't even type very well anymore. I can, but it's a real chore. Yet, this is what makes Private Label Rights such a great thing for me.

Furthermore, I'm not one of the Internet marketing "gurus" out there. I'm just a regular guy and I'm not going to sell you a bill of goods and feed you all the hype that's chock full of stuff and nonsense. You don't need that and I don't want to give it to you. This isn't instant riches... because I'm sure that both you and I know that there isn't really any such thing as instant riches or overnight successes. (I have met a few people who have attained "overnight success" and the fame accompanying it— it only took them a couple of decades of hard work).

Is making money from PLR hard work? If you want it to be successful it is. Hey, come on. If it wasn't work, we'd call it something else. But just because you have to work at it, it doesn't mean it isn't fun; it doesn't mean that it isn't worth it; and it certainly doesn't mean that you won't make money from it. There are many people that I have met since I've been enterprising online that are making a lucrative living from PLR, and although I'm not a millionaire, I'm not suffering because of it. I've made my mistakes along the way but that's what `PLR Payday` is all about. Sharing with you what I've learned so that you won't have to make the same mistakes I have made.

I have only been in online marketing for less than a year and were it not for my true and primary calling as a preacher of the gospel, I could easily transition to working this job 30 to 40 hours per week to provide for a future retirement, or even 5 to 10 hours per week once I've retired in order to bring in some supplemental income to really enjoy some quality time and fun

PLR PAYDAY

in the sun with my wife.

So what does this mean for you? I told you all of that to tell you this: if I can do this, you most certainly can.

You see, with private label content you can become an instant author without ever having to type a line of text yourself!

Plus, there is an abundance of other content types online that come with private label rights, which extends your options with the kind of material you can resell for 100% profits. That's right! Every cent is yours to keep! These options include:

- Videos
- Reports
- Full Courses
- eBooks
- Articles
- Website Designs

LET'S MAKE SOME MONEY USING PLR

- Pre-made Membership Sites
- WordPress Themes
- Complete Turnkey Websites (*with sales pages!*)
- And much, much more!

Regardless of what you're interested in, there's bound to be private label content available in that market or niche. In fact, chances are pretty good that you can even find high quality private label content in some of the most obscure markets online!

PLR PAYDAY will show you exactly how you can take advantage of the power of private label to build your very own profitable online business, plus I'll reveal the exact formula I use so that you can maximize the value of *your* PLR content in the same way, so that you can purchase a single package of content once, and produce it in a number of different ways, making you even more money from the same content!

Are you ready? Of course you are. You've purchased this book. How silly of me. So, as they used to say back in the day in Alabama, "Let's get crackin'!"

ALL ABOUT YOUR PLR LICENSE

Before you start using PLR content, it's extremely important to make sure you understand the license terms that apply to private label content. You certainly don't want to risk any legal troubles that could eat up your profits.

Some of the things you need to pay attention to in a PLR license include:

 Whether or not you can edit the content (usually you can, otherwise the content is known as *resale rights*)

 Whether you have the right to claim you wrote the content

ALL ABOUT YOUR PLR LICENSE

✓ How the content can be used (sometimes it can be broken up; sometimes not; and sometimes it can be sold in certain ways and not others)

You may also want to pay particular attention to whether or not the seller has set a minimum price. Some sellers request you sell a product for a certain amount. While this can't typically be enforced legally, it's best if you follow the seller's wishes.

I will typically shy away from PLR content that is priced way too high. In marketing, when it comes to copywriting, sales pages, and perceived product value, you have to be careful because there are some pretty unscrupulous wheeler-dealers out there. Keep your head about your shoulders, don't give in to the hype or make any purchases based on a purely emotional trigger and you'll be fine. Sometimes you'll find something that you know you "just have to have"— that is the time when you want to do your most thorough research. Believe you, me— I've learned the hard way; making a simple purchase and finding out two days after the 30-day, no questions asked, money back guarantee, that there was a Master Reseller site that had the product, at a fraction of the cost... *with* private label rights!

A great book for understanding the marketer's mindset is Liz Tomey's *Profiting with Words*. Liz's book is great, not only for understanding what marketing is all about, but she gives us all the little tricks and trinkets that help us to become savvy shoppers as well.

> *Profiting with Words,* is a must read in my humble opinion, and I'll provide a link in the Bibliography and Resources sections of this book so you can get it at a special discount.

Not all private label releases offer the same licensing rights, and it's important that you always confirm what rights you have, and exactly what you can and cannot do with the material, prior to distributing it yourself.

For example, there are many variations of private label licensing, including:

▶ Personal Private Label (non transferable)

▶ Transferable Private Label

▶ Unrestricted Private Label

ALL ABOUT YOUR PLR LICENSE

Certain private label developers will allow buyers to give away the private label content as long as it's contained within a paid membership site, while others prevent the buyer from giving it away at all, and must be sold.

You need to be clear on the terms that are in place, so that you eliminate any risks of violating the terms of service attached to your purchase.

To start, if at all possible, you should try to avoid unrestricted private label packages. With these PLR releases, there is no limit in place preventing an unlimited number of people from selling or distributing the product. You'll want to avoid it because most unrestricted private label content can be given away for free. And, guess what: there's a whole lot of it out there, which you could use as your own bonuses when selling your PLR products and content.

Consider the obstacle of trying to sell content that is being mass distributed throughout your niche at absolutely no cost. Why would people purchase it from you when they could easily download the information from a different source at no cost?

The highest quality private label will come with limited licenses. What you want to do is find a developer releasing fewer than 100 copies. Furthermore, you want to make sure that the content can be sold but cannot be given away unless it is being included in a paid membership site.

By doing this, not only will you not have to worry about the content being distributed for free, but you also know that you are only one of a small group of people who will ever be able to sell it at all.

When it comes to your licensing rights, you want to purchase PLR content that allows you to...

 Sell It with Personal, Non-Transferable Rights

With these licensing rights, you will be able to sell personal rights to the completed product, but will not be able to sell the content with private label rights. This is exactly what you want because you are definitely not interested in giving your customers the right to pass on the material to others, but instead, they are purchasing a copy of a finished product for their own personal use.

Modify It

Most private label content (in fact, the majority of it) allows you to modify and edit the content in whatever way you wish, including using portions of the content in other information products you develop.

This is where combining private label material can be an exceptionally easy way of creating your very own "exclusive" release.

What you would do is purchase three to four PLR eBooks on your chosen topic. You would then go through each book, extracting the best information from each one. This could end up being nearly the entire document, or only a few chapters.

After this, you would then combine the entire collection of content into one extensive eBook, available exclusively to your customers. It's unlikely that any other competitor will create the same collection as you, and there you have it, an awesome opportunity to provide your customers a unique, original product.

This also allows you to create lengthier eBooks on your subject matter in the event that you find it difficult to locate a single eBook covering the subject in depth. This alone provides a great deal of value to your content and makes your book or eBook that much more marketable.

You need to make sure that when you combine content from multiple sources that you read through each chapter carefully, so that you can weave the content together in a logical sequence without becoming repetitious. You want your content to flow smoothly so that it's easy for the reader to understand and digest.

 Choose Your Own Price Point

Many private label developers set a fixed price on what they believe their PLR product should be sold for. This is to protect the integrity of the product and to ensure that it retains its value.

Make certain that you are given flexible rights with your PLR license because you want to set your own price on your product, not being restricted to specific price limits.

If you are concerned about your license rights, make sure you contact the developer directly with your questions. In many cases, they will also be open to negotiating more flexible licensing rights, for an additional cost.

Sell It as Your Own

You want to be able to put your own name on your PLR product and call it your own.

Try not to confuse Master Resale Rights with Private Label Rights. With Master Resale Rights (known as MRR), you are rarely permitted to change the content at all; and typically, neither are you allowed to sell it under your own name.

In fact, the primary purpose of MMR content is to provide you with a completed product to sell, without having to do any modifications or improvements to the product.

The downside to using Master Resale Rights material, however, is that you are promoting someone else's brand. Since you can't change the content, or add your name into the material, (unless it's sold as "re-brandable content"), you are potentially funneling your customers to the developer. I may not be as bright as a small appliance bulb, but I do know that if I can get it cheaper at the source, that's where I'm going to go. Your customers will figure that out as well.

You should also think of it this way: using PLR is protecting you from the prying eyes of the competition. With private label content you are keeping the source of your content confidential so that you're not just handing the keys to the store to your competitors. If you put out a great product in your niche, the competition will certainly want to know where you got it from if they suspect it was PLR.

Master Resale Rights products makes the announcement loud and clear. "Hey, you want to know where I'm getting my material? Here it is!" It won't be long before you find the very same product offered on another website just like yours discounted a few dollars, taking away sales that may have very well been yours.

By advertising the developer of MRR products, which isn't a bad thing— they need to feed their families too— nevertheless, you are detracting from the marketing and promotion of your own business. If you're in this as a business, whether full time or part time supplemental, you don't need to spend your time, and money if you're advertising, building someone else's brand. That time could be put to better use building your own brand.

CREATE TOP QUALITY INFO PRODUCTS

Consider the possibilities. If you knew exactly how to take existing content and transform it into a brand new info product that you could sell as your very own without ever having to lift a finger in developing anything yourself, what could you do with that kind of knowledge? What could you do with the kind of free time that may afford? Granted, if you're just starting out on a new business venture, you will not have a lot of free time for a month or two, but once you find your way around Internet marketing on the World Wide Web, it will get better.

This is exactly how thousands of online entrepreneurs penetrate new markets without ever having to invest a lot of time and money into creating their own products from the ground floor up. They simply take existing material, rework it so that it's essentially a fresh new product and sell it for 100% profits.

But it gets even better: you can build an entire network around private label material just by tapping into the highest quality sources online and spending a bit of time revamping the material so that it represents your own brand and professional style.

There is no shortage of exceptional quality private label material online for developing your very own info products, and even if you have never worked with PLR content before, you will be pleasantly surprised at just how incredibly simple the process really is.

To begin, regardless of your niche, there is bound to be private label material readily available. From looking for love matchmaking interests to eliminating love handles, there are articles, reports and raw material to work with. It's truly an information goldmine out there.

> As I mentioned before, there's no such thing as an instant riches or an overnight success when it comes to laboring by the sweat of your brow. If you have made a commitment to begin a new venture, like a PLR Business, if you have a family, talk it over with them; let them know that a start up for any company would require some overtime and extra effort. Get them on board and you will find support during times that might be a bit more stressful were they not encouraging you in this.

PLR PAYDAY

One thing to keep in mind, however, is that when using private label content to create your own info product, you need to spend some time tweaking the content.

Remember what I told you about work? We used to have a saying in the Navy diving community: "The only easy day was yesterday." But let's throw another old saying in there if you don't mind; one that you've probably heard before: "If you're doing something you love, you'll never have to work a day in your life."

I hope you don't mind the little side trips, but I have to tell you that I have rarely worked a day in my life, being now fifty-almost-two-years-old. "How's that?" you ask. I made my living doing something I loved. I've wanted to be a Navy frogman since I was seven years old. I was in the Navy for a decade and a half and guess what I did… yup, you got it, I was a Navy diver (*hooyah*, deep sea!). After one too many knee surgeries from an extra-curricular activity of kick-boxing, I was honorably discharged with a medical disability… but in those last few years, the Lord was planting seeds in my heart to preach, and I went right from Japan to the Philippine mission field. I loved serving the Lord Jesus on the mission field but God was preparing me through those experiences to pastor a congregation of born-again believers, so pastor a church, I did… and do so to this day. Yet, as mentioned earlier, the economy struck and I found I had to supplement my income in another way. I can honestly say that I love doing this, too.

If through this book, I've been able to help you reach some financial goals, then I have an unspeakable joy that far exceeds any price tag placed on any of the books I have written (or rewritten from PLR content).

I wrote all of that to say this: if you think you may be stuck on what niche, market or subject area you can build your business upon, take an inventory right now from within and ask yourself what you are most passionate about. Brainstorm if need be. Write everything down on a pad of paper, then once you're satisfied that you've got some ideas, do an Internet search of your topic. Check that number just below the address bar. You may find that your passionate niche is one that several million people have "Googled," "Yahoo'd," "Bing'd," or "Ask'd" about.

So, it's time to roll up the old shirt sleeves and get to work.

It's never a good idea to use PLR content in its original form, because despite the quality, it can still be improved by simply going over the material, eliminating unnecessary information, and of course, injecting your own personal style and brand into the content.

You also want to modify the content so that it is not identical to what other people are selling. You'd be surprised at just how many people fail to make simple changes that would improve PLR content, and by spending just a bit of time making the info product your own, you will be able to use existing material to develop a brand new release.

To help you get started, here is a check-list of things you should do when using private label content to create your own info product:

 Review the Material

If you are planning on using a private-label-based eBook, make sure that you read over the content yourself so that you can get a feel for the overall quality, as well as for the flow of the material. Don't assume that the material is high quality and can be used "as is" without personally reviewing the entire document. Rare is the case when you will find content that needs absolutely no revision; and as mentioned previously, if you are branding your business, you'll want it to have your own personal touch-- and that is never included in any PLR content.

If you are going to give the content your personal stamp of approval and feature it as your own info product, you want to make absolutely certain that the info product represents your brand in a positive way.

After all, you are going to make money selling this product and you want to minimize the number of refund requests. You also want to begin developing an online presence as someone who is a reliable source for quality information.

 Editing the Material

Many types of PLR content must be edited before you use it. Sometimes the license requires this, but even when it doesn't, you should edit PLR content anyway.

There are several important reasons for editing PLR:

 PLR articles used on the web will be considered duplicate content and may not rank well (or at all)

 Books and video content will not be worth as much if they are widely distributed

 If people buy something from you and have already seen it elsewhere, they will be likely to

ask for a refund

If you submit PLR content to certain places, you may get banned

You won't be able to edit videos very much, but it's very important to make changes to articles before you use them online, and you should also consider changing eBook content before selling it.

 Change the Product Title

This is very important, especially if you want to shield the fact that your info product was originally private label material. Consider what titles you could use that would attract attention.

 For example: Rather than using the title your PLR eBook came with, *Complete Guide to Dog Obedience*, consider *Good Boy! The Pros' Secrets for Training Your Dog to Trust & Obey.*

Here's another one: Instead of using the PLR title *27 Money Saving Ways to Spend Your Holidays*

in Hawaii, try *Maximize & Economize Your Hawaiian Vacation with over 2 Dozen Tips & Tricks for Your Trip*

Remember, the title of your product will appear on the graphics that you use to represent it on your sales page, as well as within all your advertising campaigns.

 Change the Table of Contents

The first thing I do after reviewing a potential private label product that I am going to rebrand as my own is to change the Table of Content titles.

We want to avoid changing the actual structure of the table of contents, otherwise the content might not make sense or flow properly; nevertheless, by simply changing the titles of every chapter within the info product we have eliminated the chance that someone will identify our product as originating from PLR.

Now, here are some actual PLR titles to a product I was considering using in the past, but never used it in order to give my attention to some other projects:

PLR PAYDAY

TABLE OF CONTENTS

1. Increasing Your Web Traffic Starting Now! 6
2. How to Generate Traffic Using Only Free Methods 9
3. Search Engine Optimization and Why You Got to Use It 12
4. How to Use a Tell-A-Friend Script to Drive Traffic Today 15

Compare the titles on page 24 with those below:

TABLE OF CONTENTS

1. Now is the Time to Increase Your Web Traffic Flow! 6
2. Apply These Simple Methods to Generate Free Traffic................. 9
3. SEO: What is It and Why You Need It 12
4. Tell-A-Friend Scripts Drive Traffic Simply and Quickly... 15

All I've done is quickly taken each of the chapters (there were actually more in the original product but these are enough to give you the idea) and assigned a new title that is relevant to the information in that chapter. I have not yet made any structural changes to the content itself. That will come next.

Even though it would be helpful to have a talent like the rhyme-master, Al Sharpton, you actually don't have to be catchy or full of alliterations when you make your titles. They need to convey the same thought in different words.

If you're rewriting them with a program such as MSWord in Microsoft Office (I know, I know, I need to switch from PC to

Mac— working on it), then you're equipped with tools that enable you to hover over a word with your mouse, right click, and find a synonym for that word. That is very helpful for creating new chapter titles... and for editing too.

By spending only a few minutes rewriting the chapter titles for a new project, it will certainly help to make the eBook harder to identify as private label content.

 Edit Content

This step takes a bit more time, but it's an essential part of re-branding private label content into your own information product. While you don't have to rewrite the entire document, you should spend some time re-phrasing and in some cases, explaining the material more clearly.

Depending on the quality of the private label content that you are using, only slight editing may be required, and if you are unable to do this yourself, you can easily outsource the work to a freelance writer for a nominal fee.

If the quality of your material doesn't require a lot of improvement, however, you should still modify the content just enough so that it represents your particular style. Your brand is what makes you stand out. Even if you're not in a niche that is unique, anyone can do what you're doing, but no one can be who you are. So, you just continue to be you, and be the best you possible.

Let's consider some editorial changes...

- When you read through the material, does it sound like something you would write?

- Could you explain it in your own words better or more clearly than the author did?

- What could you add to the document to expand the information, or more fully expound upon it so that the reader better understands the topic?

Your style is going to be different from that of another, and it's important that you incorporate your own voice and phrasing into the eBook itself.

> "Every man's life ends the same way. It is only the details of how he lived and how he died that distinguish one man from another."
> ~Ernest Hemmingway

You want people to become familiar with you, your brand, and ultimately your message. The style and methods of another will not necessarily reflect your own, and you should take the time to blend in your own voice to any existing content you choose to use.

Likewise, you should be attentive to words or phrases that you wouldn't normally use. Those little things make a difference. Not long ago, I read to a family member a portion of a chapter I had written from an original book, and then read a portion from a chapter I had edited from PLR content. My family member couldn't tell the difference. You're on the right track when this begins to happen.

You'd be surprised just how much of a difference this will make in helping you grow your own brand and become an authority to customers who will be able to instantly recognize your style in future eBooks.

There are always improvements that you can make so that the info product becomes more aligned with your personal style. You want people to see consistency in your work and in every info product you release. One way of ensuring this happens is by always proofing and editing every PLR document you use.

A unique style is in the details, and it doesn't take too many of them to provide a rhythm in your editing that will make it so that, in no time, a developer might chance upon your eBook, read it because the title caught his or her eye, and send you an email to say, "Great job editing the content! If I didn't know it was mine because of _____ sentence in all my work, I'd swear someone else wrote this book!"

 Add Those Finishing Touches

When it comes to finishing the info product so that it's ready for distribution, you want to be sure to add your name, and website URL to the product. You should also edit the header and footer of the document so that it includes your product's new title.

You'll want to ensure that you have changed any affiliate links contained within the eBook to your own links. Most PLR developers do not include affiliate links in their content; nevertheless, make sure that this little detail hasn't been overlooked.

Links left in your content of which you are unaware may have the potential to become a big problem if the link is to a site that you do not endorse, or moreover, disapprove. Remember, I continue to mention branding, and branding means that the little things you do, just as much as the big picture, speaks volumes about who you are, the products you provide, and the services you supply.

CREATE TOP QUALITY INFO PRODUCTS

You should also consider hiring an experienced graphic designer to create eCover graphics to represent your product and give it a higher perceived value. An original, professionally designed eCover (that looks like a regular book), or an entire mini-site design for your website, will go a long way in making your product stand out when it comes to promoting your products. I actually do most (not all) of my own designs, but I have included some resources in the Resources section of this book.

After all of that, proofread your work one last time and make a quick perusal (or thorough examination if need be) of the elements associated with your product, minisite, blogs, marketing emails, etc., and then give it your stamp of approval.

SEEKING QUALITY SOURCES

Now that you know the kind of work that is before you, you can set out to look for sources that will provide you with the kind of high quality content you can use to create your info product. While there are literally thousands of private label distributors online, you really want to spend some time evaluating the products to ensure that you are using the highest quality material available online.

REMEMBER: Branding means High Quality!

Locating PLR is simple. Locating quality PLR is another matter entirely. Most PLR content is poorly written, and so widely distributed that it's difficult to make money with it. Believe me—been there, done that, and bought the tee-shirts for my entire family and a few of the neighbors, too!

SEEKING QUALITY SOURCES

I advise never buying extremely underpriced content. I understand it's tempting when you see 25 products for $17, or a product for 99 cents, but one of the reasons the content is so inexpensive is because it's being sold to thousands of people. It is much harder to make money with content when it is so widely distributed. Another reason that it has such a low price is because its content is inferior... because, frankly, it was done on the cheap for a quick buck.

Instead, look for content that is strictly limited. Buy from suppliers who are trusted, because they aren't likely to want to ruin their reputations by selling far more than they claim they will.

If possible, get a small sample of the content before you buy. This is especially important if you have never bought from the seller before. You want to ensure the content is readable, because some sellers may be outsourcing their content to people who speak English as a second language, which may often result in content that is difficult to read, and for all intents and purposes, practically useless.

In this game, you want to sell to sell again. You want customers coming back, and also recommending you to their friends, and poor quality is not the way to do it. Certainly, I have been able to successfully turn some articles around; nevertheless, it finally occurred to me that I shouldn't have to waste my time correcting poor grammar. Although it is not true in every case with regard to PLR, that old saying is still a pretty good rule of thumb: "You get what you pay for."

When choosing private label to use in creating your info product, you want to purchase enough material to use for your first eBook as well as being able to create follow up offers. You will also want various types of private label content, including:

- eBooks
- eReports
- Articles
- Autoresponders
- Video Tutorials
- eCourses & Newsletters
- Worksheets

SEEKING QUALITY SOURCES

▶ Case Studies

While it's likely that you will be able to find private label material to use in your entire campaign, in the event that you struggle to locate quality content for your entire back-end system, you can use what resources you have and outsource the rest of the material.

Let's take a closer look at how to use these different content formats:

 eBooks

You will probably want to purchase a handful of PLR eBooks on your chosen topic, so that you can determine the one that is the top of the lot and pick of the litter. I will also show you how to create a winning product by using a combination of PLR eBooks that carry a higher perceived value and are not likely to be offered in the exact same way by the competition.

 eReports

These PLR reports or eReports will be used to build your mailing list. The eReport is basically offered as a carrot before the cart, so to speak. It provides incentive for your visitors to subscribe to your email list that is set up as an autoresponder.

 Articles

You should use your PLR articles in a number of different ways. They will be used as content for your blogs or websites. You will also use them in your autoresponder campaigns, which are set up through your email service. You will also use this content in article marketing as well as other advertising campaigns.

 Autoresponders

While it's not as easy to always find high quality private label autoresponders for every niche market, there are a number of developers in the market who release "pre-written list building packages." These feature a number of follow up broadcasts and autoresponder messages that you can use in your email service, whether you use Aweber, Mail Chimp, Constant Contact, etc. Personally, I use Aweber, but that's entirely up to you.

SEEKING QUALITY SOURCES

In the event that you can't find a PLR provider offering autoresponder messages in your niche, you can always use articles to jump-start your list building, until you can outsource the work to a reliable freelancer.

Keep in mind that using private label material to create your first info product is a cost effective, simple alternative to hiring experienced writers. Once you have launched your first successful info product campaign, you should consider focusing future projects on original and exclusive content.

You can continue using private label material later on, but primarily as bonus products to your main offer.

When choosing what private label you are going to use, there are a few things to keep in mind, including:

- Market Saturation
- Licensing Limitations
- Number of Licenses Offered
- Follow Up Products

☞ Quality of Products

Let's take a closer look at each aspect to choosing a quality private label:

⭐ Market Saturation

What this means is that you will be evaluating the number of copies currently being distributed online.

Since it is private label content, it's likely that you are going to find it being sold on various websites; yet, you want to try to focus on content that is not heavily saturated, otherwise it may be difficult to sell it in venues and marketplaces such as ClickBank, ClickSure, DigiResults, JVZoo, PayDotCom, etc.

One way of minimizing the amount of competition in the marketplace is by choosing private label content that is only being offered to a limited number of people.

For example, many developers will create an eBook and allow only 25 people to purchase a license enabling them to resell it. While these licenses will cost more than unlimited private label

SEEKING QUALITY SOURCES

releases, the value is much higher since there will be a smaller group of competitors selling the same material.

Be very careful with this. To be absolutely sure, contact the PLR developer first and verify just how many licenses are being sold. Try to work with established writers who aren't likely going to risk their reputations by selling a higher number of licenses than they had advertised.

Regardless of the number of licenses being sold, you should always run a quick check to determine how many copies are already being distributed. Since most people do not change the product's original title, it is relatively easy to get a good idea as to how many people are already selling the product. Simply do a Google search.

Go to www.Google.com and enter the title of your product, enclosing the text in quotations like this:

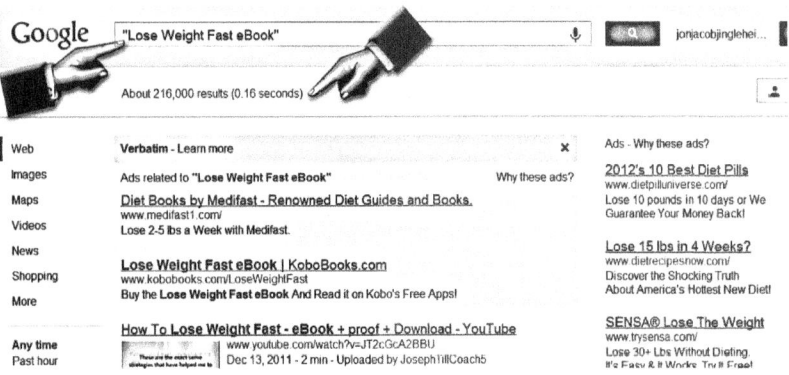

The image on page 38 is just to give you an idea where to look. When you run your search on your computer, you can see it pretty easily. There have been some changes to the Google search engine in recent months, but it is no less effective to provide you information necessary for your research in building a campaign.

In the example, I typed in "Lose Weight Fast eBook," keeping the text in quotations (just the first thing that came to mind). The bottom finger points to the results of that search, which it derived in 0.16 seconds. In less than two-tenths of a second, that very focused search for "Lose Weight Fast eBook" resulted in 216,000 hits on sites that contain that phrase. Granted, some sites and blogs may include that phrase more than once on a page or article, but it gives you an idea, with a specific figure, the popularity of the term.

In order to get more specific with regard to the title of your PLR eBook, you can look at the column on the left side under the words that say "Web" and in that section you'll find the word, "Shopping" between the words "New" and "More" (again, you will see this easily on the left hand column when you open www.google.com on your own computer).

When you click on the link, "Shopping," it will expand to reveal several options for searching your term. This will help you to see if the title you have selected is used elsewhere.

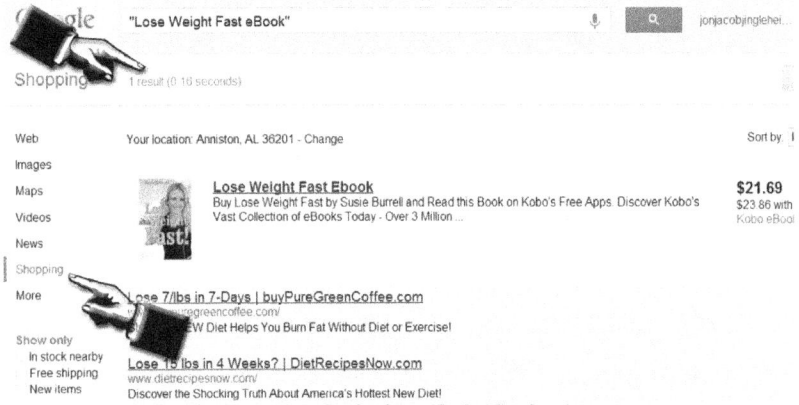

Here, our search has produced a book that has the exact same title as your proposed eBook. This one is sold on Kobo for $21.69. Just because this book has a title that is exactly like the one you intended to use, doesn't mean you can't use it. Your PLR content will more than likely be quite different from what this author has written.

In fact, I purposely used PLR Payday for this book because there is a PLR eBook titled *PLR Payout*. By giving my book a similar name, I'm hoping that those searching for the PLR book will come to my sites for this book. At least I'm hoping that is what happens. It may just backfire on me... but I certainly hope not.

You can also enter a portion of the eBook content to find similar results; or the Table of Contents itself, both of which will help you get a better idea as to the number of copies in circulation.

One more thing that could be helpful is to conduct a search in Amazon.com for your eBook, content, or Table of Contents. Do the results yield the very same words as the PLR you are about to purchase? See how it ranks. If many similar titles are ranked well with Amazon.com, it may suggest that it's not a saturated market, but instead, one that is very popular. On the other hand, if there are a large number of books listed in the niche you're considering, yet, not even the number one book listed is in the top 100, that may suggested that the market is saturated, as these titles just aren't moving.

 Licensing Limitations

Once again, we DO NOT WANT unrestricted master resellers' right products for our PLR business. Though we had mentioned what we don't want, it is a very good thing to have a grasp on what it means to have products with licensing limitations.

On the next page I've included an excerpt from a developer, who spells out specifically what you can and cannot do with the product he has developed.

SEEKING QUALITY SOURCES

As a PLR Owner You Can...

♥ You Can Use This Product Yourself

♥ You Can Sell This Product at a Price Point Determined by You.

♥ You Can Give Away The Product (NOT The Source Code Files) To Your Subscribers, Members or Customers as a Bonus or Gift.

♥ You Can Add This Product to a Membership Site or Bundled Within a Product Package as a Bonus.

♥ You Can Modify the Product Anyway You See Fit To Add/Remove Content or Make It a Brand New Unique Product, Break It Up Into Articles, Email or Online Course Lessons.

♥ You Can Rebrand, Rename, Redesign The Product & Create New Graphics to Call It Your Own.

As a PLR Owner You Cannot...

PLR PAYDAY

🚫 You Cannot Give Away, sell or transfer the Private Label Rights to any third party.

🚫 You Cannot Use the names of _____ or _____ in any of your marketing, advertising or promotional campaigns.

🚫 You Cannot Claim Copyright.[1]

🚫 You Cannot Sell Private Label Rights, Master Rights or Resell Rights to this Product in any form.

 Number of Licenses Offered

We've already considered briefly that you and I desire a limited number of licenses offered for your PLR business, but what

---

[1] This means that you cannot register the PLR content with the Copyright Office in the U.S.A., or another copyright agency operating under the guidelines of the particular country wherein it resides. This certainly doesn't mean that you must place the developer's copyright information on your product and associated websites, etc.; that would rather contradict the entire purpose of PLR material. It just means that you and I cannot claim the material as our own original work. The content would have to be substantially and significantly changed in order for a claim to be made.

SEEKING QUALITY SOURCES

must you and I look for specifically when we seek a quality PLR item, which is only offered to the next _____ customers?

Typically, the fewer products sold by the developer, the more it will cost you. Let's say that you run across an advertisement that sells a product, "But don't wait," reads the webpage, inventory is going fast and we are only selling this great product to the first fifty customers." Now, it may work one of two ways—it may be on that page in which you are making your initial purchase, or once you've made your purchase and you're directed to the download page, before the download page comes forth (or sometimes it's on the download page) this "One Time Offer" (OTO) or "One Time Special Offer" appears, giving you the opportunity to purchase the Private Label Rights (also called *White Label* because you get to put your own brand on the label). Depending upon the niche, the demand, and the product offered, the developer will specify a number to be sold and a price for those rights. At that point, your research will come into play for you to decide whether or not it is worth your while to purchase the rights.

Now, you can't just leave this to chance. Although it *can* happen, typically, your content will come with perseverance and due diligence. One of the very best ways to stay current on what's coming out, and have the opportunity to get in on a better deal through a developer that puts out his or her product

PLR PAYDAY

in a limited quantity, is to join one of the more established forums on the Internet that cater specifically to Internet marketers; and as a PLR marketer, you would fall into that category. Warrior Forum and JVZoo have email lists you can sign up for to get the latest on what has arrived. Not everything that comes into your email will be applicable, and as enticing as some of the offers may sound, unless you believe you absolutely need it, wait for what is most applicable for you business. It will save you money if you do.

Warrior Plus, although run by the same folks, is completely independent of Warrior Forum. Get an account with Warrior Plus to stay current on Warrior Special Offers (WSO).

Participation in the Forums, even just reading the reviews of products that have been offered, is a wealth of information that you should use to your advantage and help you stay current in the things that can affect your business.

ClickBrief is another resource that will provide you with a lot of good information. You might want to sign up for their eNews.

 Follow Up Products

SEEKING QUALITY SOURCES

The PLR package certainly has a higher value, and typically of higher quality, if follow up products are provided. Does the package provide PLR articles that may be used on your blog in order to promote your eBook? Do relevant, information-packed autoresponders accompany your eBook so that the customers on your email list can become more knowledgeable, and thus, make a knowledgeable decision when it comes to purchasing your eBook? Is a minisite or sales page provided in your package and is it easy to edit and upload to your hosting service?

I consider the sales page and thank you page as part of your follow up materials because these items may have an affiliate link on the site so that your customers can receive commissions for promoting your eBook. Additionally, the contact information link on the website and thank you page provide opportunities to serve your customers beyond the mere sale of the eBook. You want repeat business. Furthermore, a PLR business is an information service business. If it's just about making a buck, and has nothing to do with serving others and seeking their success, then why do it? There's plenty of other ways to make money.

Having said that, getting sales and design pages with your package isn't really all that desirable; does "branding" ring a bell? We'll talk more about that in Chapter 6, "Maximize Your

PLR Potential."

 Quality of Products

The final factor to consider in finding the PLR product that is right for you is to weigh its overall quality. If your PLR product come from a developer with whom you are unfamiliar, is he or she willing to provide a sample of the product on request? I don't know about you, but that kind of service goes a long way with me. If I can get a sample on request, it tells me that they, too, are not merely interested in making the quick sale, but cultivating a relationship with a long-term customer. It's always a pleasure doing business with real, honest-to-goodness business people.

The developer's sales pages, blog or website, and squeeze pages if applicable, are typically our first introduction to a new source of PLR. If their sales page stinks, except in the rarest of exceptions, it tells me to steer well clear of this accident waiting to happen. The quality is in the details; and if the sales page is well thought out, filled with solid information, opens in the browser easily, and allows easy access to ordering the product, more than likely you and I can expect to receive the same kind of sales page and thank-you page in our package, with PLR content that his likewise top shelf.

A website typically operates with images that contain details in its resolution of 72 pixels per inch (ppi), and sometimes 96 ppi. Anything more than that usually only succeeds in slowing down the upload time for the image to show up on your browser window. Now, if the images on the sales page or website are sloppy, grainy, pixilated, or just poor quality, that's a huge red flag, and I know I won't be making that purchase.

Finally, here's something that I've found to be quite common; it shouldn't be, but it's there so beware. I received a free bonus package once that had a great license, good content in the eBook, and some pretty good accompanying articles and autoresponders. There was only one flaw and it was a big one: more than 75% of the claims made on the sales page just were not in the eBook at all. When the sales page says, "I'll show you my tried and true methods, strategy X, strategy Y, and strategy Z..." and yet, none of those strategies are in the book, report, articles, or autoresponders, it makes you think twice about your purchase. I haven't done anything with it, but it was free... and, at the risk of sounding redundant, "You get what you pay for." It's out there so watch out. By the way, I'm making an effort to ensure I'm providing quality bonuses as well; don't want my customers bush-whacked or blind sided.

STEPPING IT UP WITH MEMBERSHIP SITES

One of the ways to leverage high quality PLR is to create membership sites. There are two main types of membership sites you can create with PLR content:

 Membership sites that sell PLR content

 Niche membership sites

 Membership Sites that Sell PLR Content

If you want to sell PLR content to other individuals with private label rights included, you'll need to be sure that every package you purchase has a reseller license. You can't automatically assume a license will allow PLR to be resold, because many do not.

You'll have to decide what type of membership site you'd like to run. You could either offer a small number of packages each month (or perhaps only one); and focus on quality, or you could deliver hundreds of packages and focus on quantity.

If you're going to do this, read the licenses very carefully. Some licenses allow resale, but do not allow membership sites; or they may have price restrictions for use with membership sites.

 Niche Membership Sites

A niche membership site can be established on any subject as your theme; and almost any type of PLR content can be used. You can add PLR articles to your membership site as general content. You can add eBooks and reports as downloads. You can also use video and audio content.

Niche membership sites generally have far less competition than PLR content sites because internet marketing is a relatively closed market. A large number of sellers are competing to sell to a relatively captive market, and most marketers are being offered dozens of PLR packages per month from various sellers.

Niche markets are different, however. In niche markets, there is practically unlimited potential. There are usually few or no membership sites in most markets.

Be sure to include a forum in your membership site. Forums allow you to have your members create content, and they inspire a sense of community that keep members paying every month just to connect with one another.

 Pricing Membership Sites

Niche membership sites generally have more members than PLR membership sites, but they cost less. Most niche membership sites are less than $20 per month, and many are as low as $5 per month. If you go above $9 per month, you're more likely to get cancellations.

Remember, attrition is a normal part of running a membership site. The average member of a continuity program stays for 3 months, but you can increase this by keeping the price low and offering timely updates with quality content.

STEPPING IT UP WITH MEMBERSHIP SITES

Always update on time, no matter what. If you are late updating, your cancellations will usually go through the roof, especially if you are longer than a week late!

PLR memberships can support a higher price point than niche sites. Many PLR sites run $97 per month or more. Yet, those sites generally have unique content that is extremely high quality and often strictly limited.

If you will be using content you've purchased resell rights to, you probably shouldn't charge more than $20 per month; however, you can add value to the products you buy and charge more. You might create new graphics or add article packages, for example. This could boost the price by a few dollars per month.

Some people want to charge the lowest possible amount per month, but there are some reasons you might not want to do that:

- You might not get enough members to make the low price worth it
- People might think your content is junk if your

price is too low

 You won't make much if you limit memberships and have a low price

Base your price on a happy middle ground between profit and gaining members.

 Membership Scripts

There are hundreds of scripts out there for creating a membership site. It can be difficult to choose between them. Nonetheless, there are others that really stand out, like…

www.MemberSpeed.com

MemberSpeed is the most comprehensive and feature-packed membership software for internet marketers today. The cost is prohibitive for many, but it works well, has a wide variety of features, and it's highly respected in the internet marketing industry. Check out the website as they occasionally offer special discounts and trials.

If you find the idea of installing script daunting, you're not alone. You may prefer using a WordPress-based membership script. Many hosting companies have Fantastico, which offers push-button simplicity for the installation of WordPress. Thus, you don't have to worry about the complexities of script installation.

There are many WordPress membership plugins available, as well. This WordPress plugin provides a number of positive benefits at an affordable price:

www.WPSalesBuddy.com

 Taking Payment

You'll need a way to accept payment for your membership site. Most people use PayPal, but other payment methods are available. I suggest PayPal because most of your members will either already have an account with them, or will be comfortable using them because they are so well-known and prevalent.

If you can't get a PayPal account, try these alternatives:

http://checkout.google.com

https://payments.amazon.com

MAXIMIZE YOUR PLR POTENTIAL

One very cost effective method of creating eBook products is by combining a series of high quality articles to produce a uniquely single item.

You can do this with private label content easily, but you can also do this by outsourcing article writing to several freelancers, and stringing the material together to form your info product.

Since it's always more affordable to hire article writers than eBook writers (even though the content is very similar), just by doing a bit of the work yourself in collectively combining the material into one product, you can create a very special and exclusive product that will cost you much less than it would were you to hire someone to write an eBook.

MAXIMIZE YOUR PLR POTENTIAL

When you purchase private label rights to eBook packages, quite often you will discover that you receive a complete website package, including a design and sales page.

I strongly recommend that you do not use the design or sales page that is included with the package. Instead, I suggest hiring an affordable designer to create a custom website template for your product (unless of course you have the skills to design a sales page— who knows? I'm learning to do it, and some you may just have that skill as well. If you do, that's a big plus). You want to begin building your own online identity in your market, and in order to do that, you need a website that is unique to your offer and established brand awareness.

When it comes to using any sales pages that may come bundled in with your PLR purchase, I once again, suggest not using the material "as is", however it can be very helpful in providing you with a guideline that summarizes what the product is all about. Use this information to write your own sales page, or if you are hiring a copywriter, provide your writer a copy of the sales page as a reference guide.

This will cut down on the time it takes to create the sales page, and can save you money in the end.

Every part of your website should be unique, aside from the product itself. Use private label content as the basis of your info product, but everything around it should be wrapped in your own personal style, from the design of the site to the sales page content.

Beef Up Your Product Value

One great use for PLR is to increase the value of other products you are selling. For example, if you create a product on making money with blogging, you might use a PLR guide on keyword research as a bonus. That way, the bulk of your content is unique, but you can bulk up the size and value of the package without additional work.

Any type of PLR will work as bonus offerings; however, it is especially valuable to include eBooks, videos, and audio materials. Videos will add the most value, especially if they are quality videos and related to your product. Most people see video content as much more valuable than written content, so they are willing to pay more for products that include it.

This could be used for niche marketing as well as internet

marketing products; yet, keep in mind that many internet marketers will have seen these packages before. Therefore, in order for your package to have true value, you must either edit them, or at least create new graphics to make them look unique if you want people to believe they are valuable.

 Product Launch Bonuses

Another creative way to use PLR is to offer it as bonuses to people who buy a product through your affiliate link. People may get dozens of emails about the same product launch. Some buy from the first email they get, but many do not. They may decide to wait for reviews about the product, or they may not have the money to buy it at that time, or they may wait to see who offers the best bonuses.

Many marketers offer huge bonus packages in order to entice people to buy through their affiliate link instead of someone else's. Since a lot of people know this, they will often wait until they find a bonus they really like before they make their purchase.

You could increase your affiliate income significantly by offering a massive package of PLR, either with resale rights (if it fits with the product) or with personal rights.

BUILD YOUR LIST

As you probably know, email marketing is extremely profitable. It has been said that the average email marketer makes approximately $1 per subscriber per month. Therefore, the larger your list, the more money you stand to make.

Of course, growing your list isn't a Sunday stroll through the park. PLR content can make the job a little easier. There are two main ways to use PLR content to make life a little easier for you when it comes to building and managing a list.

 Giveaway Reports

Some PLR content providers offer reports that can be used to build an email list. You offer these reports to people for free who join your list. Some developers even offer squeeze pages to entice people to subscribe so you won't have to create one yourself.

You can set the autoresponder of your email provider to deliver the report immediately to people who join. Just set the first message people receive when they subscribe to have a link to the report.

 Articles for List Content

If growing your list is difficult, managing one can be even harder. A lot of people can't think of anything to say to their list members, and as a consequence, they only email with advertisements. But this will make your list members tune you out or even unsubscribe.

You need to contact your list with content at least two or three times for every one time you send out an advertisement. The higher quality the content you send your subscribers, the more often they will actually read your messages, including those that promote products.

BUILDING WEBSITES

PLR content is perfect for building content websites like blogs, AdSense sites, etc. Articles make it fast and easy to create large websites without having to spend a fortune to outsource unique content, and without having to spend a large amount of time coming up with article topics on your own.

You must make sure you edit the content carefully to ensure it is as unique as possible. A few years ago, this would have been simple using a content spinner, or you could have simply manually rewritten the content. However, it's no longer that simple to make content unique.

Once, it was enough to make sure the content would pass a test at CopyScape.com, which would check to ensure the wording was unique. Now that search engines are improving their technology, it is said that the uniqueness of the wording is no longer enough. Today, your content must be just as unique.

The best way to accomplish this is to take multiple articles on the same basic topic and combine them while rewording the content. Here is an example:

Article #1 covers:

- Materials used to build widgets
- How to build widgets
- Dangers of building widgets

Article #2 covers:

- Sanding widgets
- Painting widgets
- How to choose colors for widgets

You could create an article combining parts of both articles, and it would be something no one else would have.

The information would be combined in a distinctive way, thus creating a completely unique and exclusive article. You might include materials and building instructions from the first article, and sanding and painting from the second. You could even take this further by creating a second article with the remaining content from both articles.

 WordPress

When I refer to WordPress here, I am referring to WordPress.org as opposed to WordPress.com. The WP.com version of WordPress was developed as a blogging platform for those who did not use or did not know how to use web hosting, FTP tools, etc. Many of the common blogging features that WP.org users have, are made available free of charge by WP.com. Extra features, such as domain name registry, video uploads, and so forth, can be purchased for WP.com; yet, the WP.com's distinctive difference is that you cannot use your blog for commercial advertisement. In other words, if you are an Internet marketer, whether an affiliate, developer, or PLR content provider, commercial ads are against the rules of use with WP.com. This is how the WP.com branch of WordPress are able to make their platform free, since the ads that do show up on WP.com sites are those who are paying WP.com for advertising. The ads on your blog will compete with those placed there by WP.com. To have an ad-free blog site on WP.com, you must pay an annual fee (at this writing the price for "No Ads" is $30).

BUILDING WEBSITES

There are advantages and disadvantages in both for the average user; however, if you're an Internet marketer, then WP.org is the way to go if you're using WordPress.

Many people choose to use WordPress as the foundation for their sites, because it is a lot easier for the average person to use than creating sites with HTML, which requires some programming or a WYSIWYG editor like Dreamweaver.

WordPress is valuable for other reasons, too. You can install plugins that increase the functionality of your site. For example, plugins can allow you to include a forum on your site, run giveaways, and much more.

Additionally, WordPress will allow you to take your articles and pre-load them into your blog in order to set the content to update automatically. You could load a month's worth of articles into the post section of your dashboard and schedule them to be published whenever you wish.

Google loves fresh content, and it tends to list sites with recent updates much higher than those that haven't been updated recently. So you can use this automatic update system to push your sites higher in the search engines with fresh articles.

RIDING THE AMAZON MARKETPLACE RIVER

Amazon would seem to be the largest retailer online today. I won't sell you on any hype, but they do a pretty substantial amount of business. Their quarterly report, ending June 30, 2012, presents that the six-month cash flow equivalents amounted to a little over $5 billion and that Amazon received a net income of $137 million. Now, there's really more to it than that, when all things are calculated and taken into consideration; nonetheless, this is a very sizeable amount of money. The figures are made publicly available because Amazon.com is a public holding and they must disclose their information every quarter to the Securities and Exchange Commission.

That's huge, but it wasn't always the case. I do remember in her early days on the Internet, Amazon almost went under.

Trust was an issue. Who really wanted to give their personal information away on the Internet? Not me; at least, not then. Now that security issues have been ironed out, it's no problem. In fact, while my family and I ministered in bush Alaska from 2002 to 2008, my wife, Lisa, purchased online all the time. We had to. Today, transactions online are as ordinary as going to the local grocery store to pick up a loaf of bread.

What does this mean for you and me as PLR marketers?

Amazon has made millionaires of many people through Kindle Direct Publishing. Indie authors can publish their content on Amazon for free and receive commissions.

Commission varies based on your price:

- $0.99 to $2.98 receives 35% commission
- $2.99 to $9.99 receives 70% commission
- $10 and up receives 35% commission

Some people prefer to price their products at $0.99 for mass exposure, despite getting only half the commission. Others choose to price at $2.99 or higher in order to make more money per sale and a higher commission. Neither way is more effective than the other; but if you're familiar with the mainstream, commercial publishing market, when Amazon Kindle provides even 35% commission, it is huge when compared to the pittance paid out by the big publishing houses… AND you can get nearly instant income, whereas the entire route through the commercial sector, with literary agents and acquisition executives and publishing editors, it's typically a year or more before your book is finally in print.

Additionally, Amazon now offers KDP Select, which allows you to promote your Kindle eBook for five days in a 90-day period so you can get reviews for your book, receive higher rankings from the promotional giveaway, and thus, receive exposure for your title.

When you couple that with a variable price scale, you can actually leverage several campaigns through a 90-day period using KDP Select, and as you monitor the trends of your sales, as they drop off, drop your price down to 99 cents until they pick up again. As your eBook grows in popularity and is approaching a peak in sales, switch the price to $2.99 for a higher commission. When you switched to the higher price, which is still very affordable, make plans for another one or two day free giveaway so that you can promote your eBook again to raise your title in the Amazon rankings for more exposure and, hopefully, more great reviews.

It is certainly something that you'll have to monitor on your own because it can change from niche to niche, from market to market, and from season to season.

Judging from the marketing reports Amazon provides, one of the strategies you'll want to build into your campaigns is the timing of when most people are typically making their purchases. The end of the traditional school year in June is a strong purchasing month, the end of August or beginning of September is also big for back to school sales and Labor Day, and of course, December for all those crazy holidays tucked into that month.

Commissions are paid 60 days after the end of a month. Now that number seems like a long time but what is meant by this is that any money you make in January would be paid to you around the end of March. It is actually better this way because if there does happen to be a return and refund, it typically takes place within the next month, and then you don't have to deal with it. All is well. Sales continue. Life is good.

Payments are made by Electronic Funds Transfer (EFT) to your bank account, or you may request a check. At the end of the calendar year, Amazon provides a Royalties and Earnings

PLR PAYDAY

Statement in the mail (even though I haven't been working with PLR that long, I have over 25 Christian titles on Amazon in paperback as well as on Kindle and Amazon has been very good about getting me my statement).

 Boating Down the Amazon with PLR Content

If you're in the Internet marketing biz, or if you're an indie publisher, you may have heard that Amazon is cracking down on PLR content, and that's true. The fact is, Amazon doesn't want hundreds of the same exact book on their site, because their users don't like to see this.

In fact, my Kindle seller's account was suspended temporarily earlier this year because of my use of public domain content in a Christian book I had written. There was an accusation made about a title I submitted. The accusation could not be substantiated at all and after an email to KDP, they replied with an apology and I am once again, in good standing.

Even if you create a totally unique cover, there is still a chance that someone may raise an objection.

Okay, here's the scenario...

Someone might buy your book along with one written by somebody else; but they notice that the content is nearly identical. They report this to Amazon thinking that one of you has infringed upon the other's copyright. Moreover, they may be quite angry with Amazon for selling two books that are alike. They won't be mad at you. Okay, maybe a little; but they'll surely be mad at Amazon for allowing this to happen. The customer feels duped and betrayed; and that's a rather reasonable rationale. How would you like to purchase a paperback book for $12.95 and another with a different title and cover for $9.95 and find out that the content is exactly the same? Now you're out $22.85 plus tax, plus shipping. So, the customer is mad at Amazon for letting this happen, both books are returned, and now Amazon is mad at you and some other PLR marketer. If you can't show proof of your original content, you may be banned from the Amazon jungle forever, and told never to be seen peddling your wares upon the mighty Internet River ever again.

It is true that many have been banned from Amazon for using PLR content, but this doesn't have to happen to you. We're not trying to get one over on them. To coin what I've said earlier in another way, the distinction is in the details.

Copyright is a rather interesting concept. The book of Ecclesiastes, in the Bible, says that there's nothing new under the sun. In other words, since the creation of the heavens and the earth, everything we see today is merely a rearrangement of the original creation. Therefore, to copyright something as an "original" work is kind of a misnomer. To put it another way, a dictionary contains most, if not all, of the words of the English language. Your PLR eBook, my book right here about PLR content, and every book placed strategically, accidentally or haphazardly on the electronic bookshelf of the Amazon River is merely an arrangement of some of those words from the dictionary.

What does that mean to you and me? Here comes that word again, "branding." Since we are branding ourselves, branding our product, and branding future products to show our distinctive flair and style, we are actually creating a unique and exclusive product.

You see, Amazon allows for even public domain content as long as you significantly alter it in order to provide additional value.

You could take a book that is in the public domain, like *The Pilgrim's Progress* for instance, and add unique illustrations to it and they would accept it. They would most probably not accept the book in its unaltered state, because there are already many copies of the book on the Amazon website. *The Pilgrim's*

Progress is a Christian allegory written by Puritan writer, John Bunyan. He used English words and expressions from the seventeenth century, words that are not easily understood today in the twenty-first century. A modern English translation of that classic work would be easily approved and accepted.

Likewise, you can do this with your PLR content. Simply alter it, make your own additions, changes and deletions, and submit it. That's what PLR is really all about: you have the basic structure of an idea and made it distinctive with your own unique voice; and as long as you've enhanced the product and added value to its content, you should be right as rain.

Here are some things that you might consider undertaking to enhance your product and add value to it...

 Add additional information

 Combine multiple books into one

 Add PLR articles to a PLR book

 Add unique illustrations or photos

Add recipes or special instructions to appropriate books

 Add in a "TIPS" section at the end of each chapter

You don't have to perform a complete overhaul of your PLR content (though that might help you to get the kind of 4 and 5 star reviews for you book); nonetheless, you should add enough of your own particular style to significantly enhance the value of what you're selling.

 Your Submission to Amazon

I've actually written a free eReport on how to be published on Amazon Kindle. I wrote it from PLR content, but that wasn't my initial intent. I received the PLR in a package with something else I really wanted, and the PLR content of the Kindle Publishing book was so horrendous, its English grammar and diction so terrible, that I ended up rewriting over 75% of the report because I had been publishing my Christian books on Kindle for quite a while. I knew the process already.

The report I have made available for free only earlier this year, is already out of date. Kindle Direct Publishing has made some changes and it is actually easier than ever to get published on Amazon.

The first step is to create your Kindle publisher's account. Do this at **http://kdp.amazon.com**

When you create your account, you'll be asked to provide payment information, and depending on your location, you will choose from different options.

For example, if you are within the United States, you can opt to receive EFT payments, which are delivered directly into your bank account. If you live within Canada, Australia or other countries where EFT is not currently offered via Amazon Kindle, your only option is to receive payment via check.

You can change your payment preferences at any time; however, if you should change your details in the middle of a regular payment, it may delay your regularly scheduled payments (that has happened to me so you'll want to watch out for the payment cycle). Double-check all of your account information to ensure that it's accurate before proceeding to the next step.

Having completed your account information, your next step is to click on "Bookshelf" from the top navigation menu. This is the first step in listing your title and publishing your eBook. Below the navigation menu you'll notice a tab at that reads "Add New Title." Click on that tab to continue.

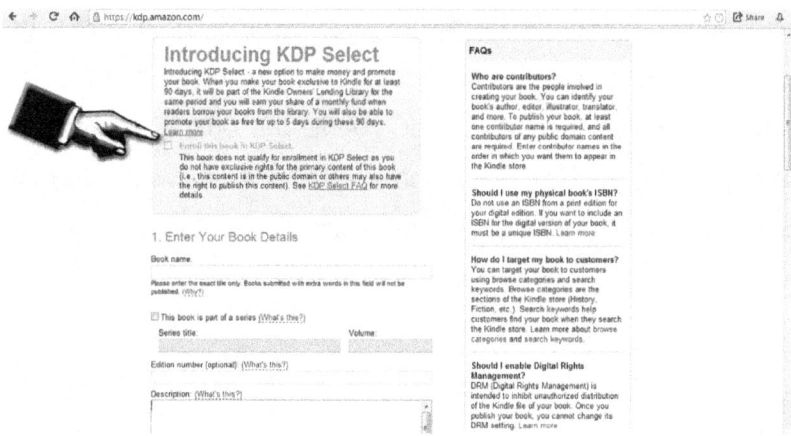

I mentioned the KDP Select program briefly as a strategy to utilize a little earlier. I suggest that before you continue in adding your title, that you check the box to enroll your title in the KDP Select program even if you never offer your book for free using the five-days-in-90 promotional giveaway opportunity. Why? For the 90-day period, anyone who is a Premium Amazon customer can borrow your book free of charge; however, there is a pool of money— it's been $600,000 every month since it started (except for one month when it was $700K)— and if you're enrolled in KDP Select, you receive a portion of the $600K, depending upon how many of your books were borrowed. In some cases, for some authors, the royalties they received from KDP Select have been greater than the royalties received for sales. The only downside to the KDP Select program is that you must agree that your eBook is exclusively sold through Amazon KDP for the 90-day period, and nowhere else. Personally, I don't see it as a downside because you're still free to pursue other markets once the 90-day KDP Select period is over... AND the potential exposure available for your book will only aid the sales when you do place it into other venues and markets.

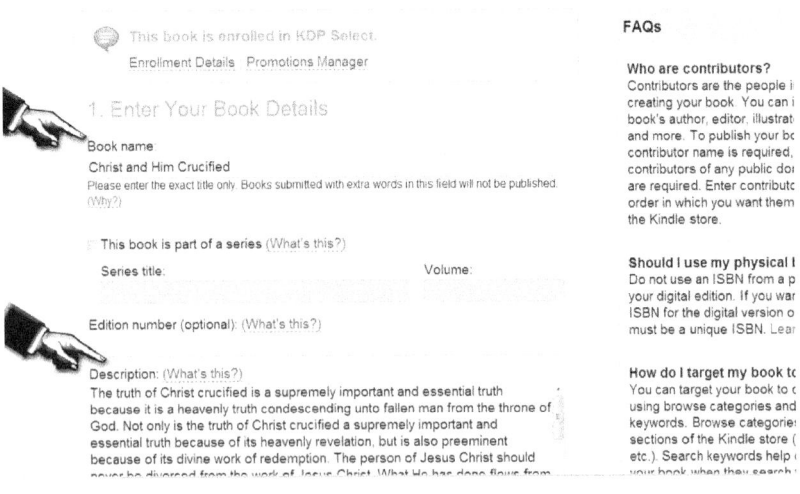

Take special note of the image I used here. I just took a simple snapshot of it by pressing "Ctrl" on the bottom left of my keyboard while simultaneously pressing "Prt Sc SysRq" on the top row of my keyboard, typically about two buttons to the right of the F12 function key. I then opened MSPaint, clicked on the

PLR PAYDAY

"Paste" clipboard icon in the top left corner of MSPaint, then saved the image as a JPEG file on my hard drive. Granted, I used Adobe Photoshop software to enhance the image to make it useable for the paperback book; nevertheless, I wanted to illustrate how the subtlety of the images provide, not only a terrific illustration for the instruction of this book, but also an example of how you make your content your very own. You'll notice that in both the former and latter images have illustrations of a finger pointing to where the attention is to be given; a unique addition if this were PLR content.

Now, here's the sweet part— I am referencing in my instruction to you a book I wrote at the end of last year. That's right! That title, *Christ and Him Crucified*, is one of my many paperback books. That's just one more element that makes any book, whether PLR, public domain, fiction, non-fiction, or what have you, stylistically unique. I guarantee you that, even if there's another PLR information book out there with very similar content, it doesn't have the distinct features that this book has. It doesn't have my personal anecdotes, nor does it have my particular, sometimes annoying, expressions (sorry about that).

Take note that the banner at the top of the page indicates that my Kindle version of *Christ and Him Crucified* is enrolled in the KDP Select Program. So you can see that I'm a Baptist pastor who practices what he preaches!

Now you may proceed to provide on this KDP web page:

- [✓] The title of your book
- [✓] A description
- [✓] Click the "Add contributors" button to add your pen name as author
- [✓] Language (probably English)
- [✓] Select that it is not a public domain work
- [✓] Add categories
- [✓] Add keywords
- [✓] Upload your book cover image
- [✓] Choosing DRM piracy prevention or not
- [✓] Upload your book

Let's take a closer look at some of these items from the first page.

PLR PAYDAY

 ## The Title of Your Book

Begin by entering in your book title. Now there's a bit of controversy over this. Some suggest keyword slugs following your main title. I also previously suggested this in a free eReport I produced, "Get Published on Amazon Kindle." Things have changed, however, and KDP tells you not to do this just below the box where you enter your title: "Please enter the exact title only. <u>Books submitted with extra words in this field will not be published</u>" (emphasis added). Moreover, in the "(Why?)" link KDP provides right after their statement, it reads:

> "In order to provide the best possible tools for independent publishers, and the best experience for your readers, Kindle Direct Publishing does not publish content that is intentionally confusing or misleading. Book titles that are unnecessarily long, or contain extraneous terms, can lead to inaccurate or overwhelming search results and impair readers' ability to make good buying decisions."

I suppose you can make a case for using your subtitle. For example, in my book PLR PAYDAY (notice how I'm branding myself!), its subtitle is, "Building Your Brand & Bringing in Bucks with Private Label Rights!" I could probably make a case with KDP for using this legitimate subtitle that is

very much a part of, and appears with the paperback book, which will be sold on Amazon.com. Nevertheless, as both Amazon, and their KDP division, has made some changes, I'll just throw another little trite cliché out there: Don't bite the hand that feeds you. My subtitle is certainly keyword-rich with regard to what this book is all about. So, for the Kindle edition, I'll just leave the subtitle off, and if it doesn't synchronize with the paperback, a quick email to KDP will get the print and electronic versions aligned for added value to the customer.

A situation where having a longer title is necessary would be if you have several slightly different versions of the same book. An example of this would be from another one of my books, so allow me to brand myself yet again…

A PURITAN BIBLE PRIMER: English Standard Version

A Puritan Bible Primer was written for Christian families to assist them in getting the basic Biblical truths to their young children; and as many English speaking Christian families have particular preferences in the version of the Bible they read and study from, I've made this book available in four formats, King James Version, New King James Version, New American Standard Bible, and of course from our example, English Standard Version.

One of the most important considerations you can possibly make when publishing any material is the title of your book. It always has been; and it is even more so today with the Internet and all the information technology in place. If your basic title is already keyword enriched, and delivers on what your title expresses, then it will be sought out and found.

 Edition Number

If your book is part of a series, you'll want to provide that information next. If it is, by making that information available, other books appearing in the same series can be linked together, stimulating sales among those who have read books in the same series.

Next, include an "Edition Number" (optional). An edition number is rarely used unless you are re-publishing a previous release, or updating your book. If this is a first publication of the material, leave this field blank.

Description and Contributors

The next step is a very important part of your book listing—providing a detailed, keyword-saturated description. You are limited to 4000 characters, so use this space wisely, providing a summary of your storyline, injecting tags that are likely to be used by people searching within your genre.

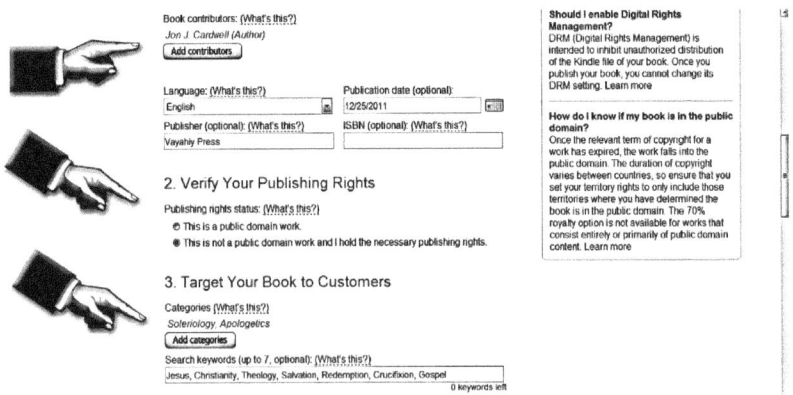

You can always update the description later should you desire; again, keeping in mind that it can take up to 48 hours for changes to appear.

If there are others who have contributed to the work, you will want to include them at this time in the space provided, which reads "Book contributors." Contributors are the authors of your book, but may also include others that you wish to credit (editors, publishers, agents, illustrators, etc). You can choose any name you wish, a real name, pen name, alias, anonymous—it's entirely up to you.

 Rights, Categories and Keywords

The next step is to verify your publishing rights. Amazon does not want anyone to publish books to which you have no legal licensing… and we've rather gone over that earlier.

Next, and this is very important, **choose your categories**. Again, like keywords, your categories will aid in searches for your eBook as well as target your particular audience. You are allowed only *two* categories per title so choose the very best ones for your genre. If you have difficulty understanding what categories are best for your work, spend some time evaluating what other authors in your genre are using and follow suit.

I really want to stress this point because when you run your campaign to offer your book free through the KDP Select program, the category you select will reflect in your rankings… and another sweet deal that comes with publishing with Amazon is that even the free downloads are included for your ranking. This provides more exposure, and hopefully, when your book is back online, with its price tag in place, you'll have more sales.

After that, you can enter in keywords. You're allowed seven (7) tags. This can include multiple words such as keyword phrases. Since only seven words or word phrases may be used, use the most relevant and most applicable to your market and genre. *Do not* include your author name, because your name will already be associated to your listing. If you are stumped on this one, again, search Amazon's book listings to find what keywords have been used with the bestselling books in your niche. Again, ensure that you are targeting the right audience with your keywords, as targeting is the key here. It's more important that you have the right eyes seeing your book than all eyes on it. All eyes might give you exposure, the right eyes get you sales.

 Uploading Your Cover Image

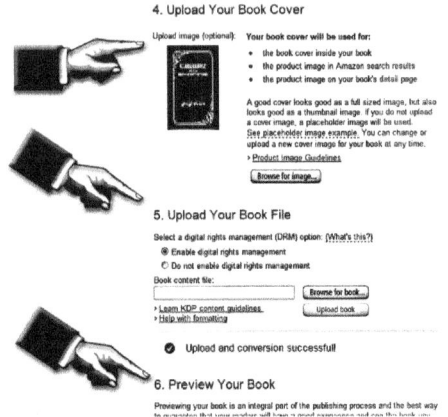

Okay, now it's time to upload your book cover. Amazon accepts book covers in two different formats— JPEG (also written JPG, or .jpeg); or TIFF (.tif or .tiff). My personal preference is JPEG.

Amazon recommends minimal compression of your cover image and the minimum recommended dimensions for your cover art are 1000 pixels on the longest side with an idea ratio of height/width being 1.6 (example 1000 x 1600). KDP prefers 2500 pixels on the longest side so 1563w x 2500h is the optimum cover. Follow these guidelines as closely as possible so that you have the sharpest image displayed, which should catch your customer's eye. Amazon wants to make the sale as much as you do so put your best foot forward here.

 ## Choosing DRM and Uploading Your Book Content

Digital Rights Management (DRM), according to KDP is...

> "intended to inhibit unauthorized distribution of the Kindle file of your book. Some authors want to encourage readers to share their work, and choose not to have DRM applied to their book. If you choose DRM, customers will still be able to lend the book to another user for a short period, and can also purchase the book as a gift for another user from the Kindle store."

KDP also mentions this in the "(What's this?)" link next to the DRM choice: "**Important**: Once you publish your book, you cannot change its DRM setting." Heed this warning because once you've made your choice for a title, it's made. There's some controversy surrounding this particular point, on whether or not it works, or is worth it; and rather than going over the issue here, you can search it out on the Internet and make your choice.

Now it's time to upload your book. As I mentioned earlier, there are some things that have changed with the Kindle Select Program. For one thing, software improvements on Amazon's side have made it easier than ever to upload a book. When I first started I had to transfer the content of my paperback book into a useable HTML format. Sometimes it was a bit confusing. Unless you have images and graphics that require special uploading considerations, if you have your book in a simple MSWord document (.doc), you can upload it and within 24 to 48 hours you should be approved and on your way to selling your Kindle eBook.

Once your book is uploaded, preview your book through the section provided. This option has been improved in the past several months as well and I highly recommend giving as much care to this step as any other step in the process. Because of the transfer of data, some features from your book may not come out the way you would like it. For example, I believe footnotes provided in the MSWord format are still problematic when the data is transferred and reformatted for Kindle, but this is the place you can spot it. Using certain symbols had also proven to be problematic in the past. It may have improved, but if it hasn't, this is where you will catch it.

Once you're satisfied and the formatting is acceptable, click "Save and Continue."

On the next page, you'll need to select your royalty percentage by following the guideline I mentioned earlier. Set a price for your book, and then have it automatically set the price for the other countries. Click the box to accept their terms and submit your book. And there you are— congratulation, you're a published author!

REAPING THE BENEFIT OF OTHER VENUES

There are several others venues available to you for submitting your content. Many of them only take fictional works, but some do allow nonfiction. The primary place for your submission is:

www.smashwords.com

SmashWords itself doesn't send a lot of traffic, however, if you carefully follow their formatting guides, your book will be accepted to their premium catalog. The premium catalog allows you to have your book distributed to other retailers, including Apple, Sony and Kobo.

SmashWords pays quarterly, approximately 30 to 45 days after the end of the quarter, so don't expect to make any money quickly with this venue. Nevertheless, the money can really add up, especially from other retailers like Apple or Sony.

Another retailer you may want to submit your eBook to is Barnes and Noble. Although Amazon has taken a lot of business away from many small and medium booksellers, Barnes and Noble is one of the large stores that continues to persevere; perhaps in part because they have been keeping up with trending technology, having an online presence, and offering their own competitive counterpart to Amazon's Kindle, the Nook. To place your book in electronic form at Barnes and Noble, you will find their PubIt! website here…

http://pubit.barnesandnoble.com

If you have trouble navigating through their website, it's not a problem if you have submitted through SmashWords. SmashWords is a provider for B&N. Most people, however, prefer to submit directly to B&N. One of the problems for a more international audience is that there are still many countries where Barnes and Noble are not accepted or vice versa.

RESOUNDING A PROMOTIONAL VOICE

Be sure to promote all of your books. Don't just submit them and ignore them. You aren't likely to get any sales if you don't do some promotion.

It works that way in the commercial publishing arena as well. Even bestselling authors, courted by the big publishing houses, have to promote their books and brand themselves. There's book signings, public appearances, yada yada yada, and the list goes on. And though they receive very lucrative paydays, the bottom line is that they're not sitting around until the next book idea comes to mind. Neither should you.

Here are some ways to promote your books:

RESOUNDING A PROMOTIONAL VOICE

 Ask for reviews from bloggers. A few will review nonfiction. I review non-fiction quite often; mostly Christian non-fiction, but I'll write a review for books written for Internet marketing, since I'm also earning a living in this market.

Who knows, if you need a review and you're reading my book right now, send me an email and if I have the time, I'll review your book. **If you've read** PLR Payday **and reviewed it on Amazon, I'll make the time and definitely review your book.** Send me an email with a PDF copy attached and I'll get it done, regardless of your niche... with the one exception: I don't read sexually explicit material... Baptist pastor, remember. ☺

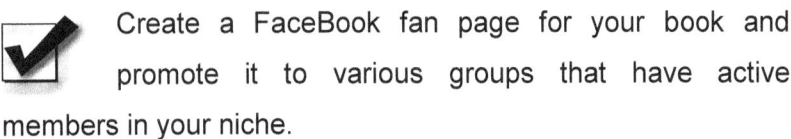 Join forums like KindleBoards.com and add your books to your signature.

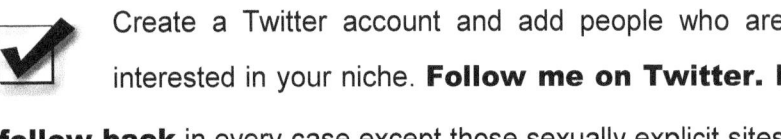 Create a FaceBook fan page for your book and promote it to various groups that have active members in your niche.

Create a Twitter account and add people who are interested in your niche. **Follow me on Twitter. I follow back** in every case except those sexually explicit sites from girls who follow me with names like Bambi offering a link that provides images that I really don't want etched into my mind. My Twitter username is "**vayahiy**."

 Write articles in your niche and submit them to article directories under your *nom de plume*, if your books use a pen name. Advertise your book in your bio box by inserting after your name, "author of _____" (providing the name of your book). If you're not on Ezine.com, that's a good place to start.

 Post comments on related blogs, using your pen name and mentioning "author of _____" in your post.

I mentioned Twitter earlier, and that is one of the first places I used "author of" in my bio information. In fact, this is how it reads:

> "*1 Corinthians 2:2; Galatians 6:14; pastor of Sovereign Grace Baptist Church; author of the bestseller, CHRIST AND HIM CRUCIFIED; CEO Vayahiy Press*"

 Finally, you absolutely must do this if you are a published author with either a paperback book with CreateSpace.com or a Kindle eBook with KDP— open a free account with Amazon's Author Central. Just go to Amazon's site, http://authorcentral.amazon.com, click on "Join Now" button and follow the instructions to set up your author's account. Go and do it. Don't make me type the "B" word again.

These are just a few ideas. Remember, the more sales you get, the higher you will jump in the ranks, and the higher you go in the ranks, the more you will sell overall.

Recapping with Resources

I've heard from someone that there are a lot of naysayers spreading the word that it is impossible to make money with PLR content. Well, I'm not sure if there are people really saying it, but I don't think it's true. I believe that if you provide an honorable service with excellent content, information that your customer certainly wants, you can either make a living from it, or you can at the very least supplement your income by it.

Certainly there's no future for your product if you just purchase it and sell it as is. That won't work and I'm telling you, I've learned the hard way. In fact, I still have reports out there sending you to sites that are still in cyberspace with content that is just like that. I'm un-branding myself from those little by little as I've learned more about PLR myself.

RECAPPING WITH RESOURCES

If anyone did make some money without reworking the PLR they purchased, it was a fluke, in my humble opinion.

If you're willing to put in a little work, you can easily make a decent dollar solely from PLR content. Take the advice you've learned in this guide and apply your own ideas and I'm sure your progress will not only be lucrative, but fulfilling as well.

When I was a kid, I used to like building models. Yes, all the necessary components were there, but it required assembly and some paint and decals. It was the paint and decals that made it intrinsically yours. You made it and it was different from your best friend's right across the way; having received the same model that year because you both talked about how great it would be to get one. His was his and yours was yours and nothing anyone could say or do would change that... except for when your little brother got mad for some reason or another and crushed your model to bits...

Yet, PLR, is similar. You've got the content, the sales page, the articles and the autoresponders, and anyone could just get some glue and slap it together. When you take the modeler's blade and scrape off the flashing, glue the pieces together carefully, sand off the rough edges, paint it with the colors that suit you, and put those decals on in the places that no one else would put them, you've got a product on your hands that actually goes beyond the model illustration. PLR is information content, and that information that you provide, that you are making a living from, is enriching the life of another human being. They are receiving value from the content, coming away from the last page knowing one more page of thought than they did before they picked up your book, whether paperback or electronic. That, my friend, is something.

In my humble opinion, if you're only in it for the sale, you'd be better off trying something else; but if you're interested in the success of others, PLR is a great way to earn some income, and help others at the same time.

 Resources to Round it Out

Let me conclude this by offering some helpful resources, of which some of you may already be aware, or even currently using, but I want to make mention of them so that those who of you that are not aware of them can avail yourselves to them.

This is certainly not an exhaustive list, but I hope that it is helpful.

RECAPPING WITH RESOURCES

 Affiliate Markets

www.ClickBank.com; www.ClickSure.com; www.DigiResults.com; www.JVZoo.com; www.PayDotCom.com

 Autoresponder Services

www.Aweber.com; www.ContantContact.com; www.GetResponse.com; www.iContact.com; www.MailChimp.com

 Domain Services

www.DomainBot.com; www.GoDaddy.com; www.NameBoy.com; www.NameCheap.com

 Hosting Services

www.1and1.com; www.BlueHost.com; www.GoDaddy.com; www.HostGator.com; www.JustHost.com

Outsource Sites

www.Fiverr.com; www.FreeLancer.com; www.ODesk.com

Some Other Helpful Resources

Free WordPress Plugins
http://wordpress.org/extend/plugins

Google Keyword Tool
https://adwords.google.com/select/KeywordToolExternal

Profiting with Words
www.piggiesgonewild.com

YouTube Keyword Tool
https://ads.youtube.com/keyword_tool

BIBLIOGRAPHY

Lou Gehrig's disease (ALS), ch.1, pg. 3
www.alsa.org

VA (Veteran's Administration), ch.1, pg. 3
www.va.gov

PLS (Primary Lateral Sclerosis), ch1, pg. 3
www.sp-foundation.org/pls.html

Profiting with Words by Liz Tomey, ch.2, pgs. 8, 9
www.piggiesgonewild.com

Warrior Forum, ch.4, pg. 45
www.warriorforum.com

Warrior Plus (Warrior Special Offers, WSO), ch.4, pg.45
www.warriorplus.com

MemberSpeed Mermbership Site Software, ch.5, pg. 53
www.memeberspeed.com

WordPress Plugins, ch.5, pg. 54
www.wpsalesbuddy.com

BIBLIOGRAPHY

PayPal, ch.5, pg. 54
www.paypal.com

Google Checkout, ch.5, pg. 54
http://checkout.google.com

Amazon Payments, ch.5, pg. 54
http://payments.amazon.com

CopyScape, ch.9, pg. 63
www.copyscape.com

WordPress, ch.9, pg. 65
www.wordpress.org

WordPress, ch.9, pg. 65
www.wordpress.com

Adobe Dreamweaver, ch.9, pg. 66
http://www.adobe.com/products/dreamweaver.html

Amazon.com Quarterly Report, ch.10, pg. 67
http://phx.corporate-ir.net/phoenix.zhtml?c=97664&p=irol-reportsOther

Kindle Direct Publishing, ch.10, pg. 68
http://kdp.amazon.com

The Pilgrim's Progress by John Bunyan, ch.10, pg. 73
ISBN: 978-1456569334

KDP Select, ch.10, pg. 77
https://kdp.amazon.com/self-publishing/KDPSelect

PLR Payday by Jon J. Cardwell, ch.10, pg. 81
ISBN: 978-1479307418

A Puritan Bible Primer – ESV by Jon J. Cardwell, ch.10, pg. 82
ISBN: 978-1456349080

SmashWords, ch.11, pg. 91
www.smashwords.com

Apple, ch.11, pg. 91
www.apple.com

Sony, ch.11, pg. 91
www.sony.com

Kobo, ch.11, pg. 91
www.kobo.com

PubIt! (Barnes and Noble), ch.11, pg. 92
http://pubit.barnesandnoble.com

KindleBoards, ch.12, pg. 94
www.kindleboards.com

Facebook Fan Pages, ch.12, pg. 94
www.facebook.com

Twitter, ch.12, pg. 94
www.twitter.com

Ezine Articles, ch.12, pg. 95
www.ezine.com

Amazon Author's Central, ch.12, pg. 95
http://authorcentral.amazon.com

ABOUT THE AUTHOR

Jon Cardwell is a wretched sinner saved by God's free and sovereign grace. He lives in Anniston, Alabama with his wife, Lisa, his daughter, Rachel, and his mother-in-law, Virginia. He is the pastor at Sovereign Grace Baptist Church in Anniston after having ministered as a missionary and as a missionary-pastor in the Philippines, California, and remote bush Alaska.

He is the author of the bestseller, *Christ and Him Crucified*, the CEO of Vayahiy Press, and the founder and overseer of Free Grace Tentmakers. Jon has also held the office of vice-chairman of the national Sovereign Grace Baptist Fellowship (2009-11), and was elected as chairman on September 13, 2011.

His Christianity has been shaped tremendously and influenced deeply by such redeemed sinners as John Bunyan (1628-1688), Charles H. Spurgeon (1834-1892), John Newton (1725-1807), and Granville Gauldin (1929-).

Some of Jon's other titles include:

Lord, Teach Us to Pray
Fullness of the Time
A Puritan Family Devotional

Jon's blogs include:

Justification by Grace
http://justificationbygrace.com

Preaching Christ Crucified
http://preachingchristcrucified.com

Free Grace Tentmakers
http://incomesupplementnow.com

Ministry websites include:

Jon J. Cardwell Online
http://jonjcardwell.net

Vayahiy Press
http://vayahiypress.com

SermonAudio
www.sermonaudio.com/vayahiy

Social media includes:

Facebook
www.facebook.com/jon.cardwell

Twitter
www.twitter.com/vayahiy

LinkedIn
www.linkedin.com/in/joncardwell

www.ingramcontent.com/pod-product-compliance
Lightning Source LLC
Chambersburg PA
CBHW061513180526
45171CB00001B/157